Psychology of Successful Sales

How to Quickly Increase Sales, Using Proven Direct Sales Strategies and Effective Marketing

Table of Contents

Preface

In this guide you will combine two powerful concepts using a step-by-step proven sales strategy with the most powerful form of conversation hypnosis ever created. If you have ever thought about a career in sales, but held off because of fear or trepidation, this guide can will teach you how to make plenty of sales, which will earn you tremendous commissions. This guide will be short on theory, and long on techniques. You'll learn the bare-bones minimum so you can get started as quickly as possible. The great thing about sales is once you find a technique that works, you'll be able to use it again and again. Within a few minutes of meeting a potential customer, you'll know precisely which structure or collection of structures to use that will maximize your ability to make a sale, and thus a commission. This guide assumes you know nothing about sales, so if you are even contemplating a sales career, this is the best place to start.

General Outline

This guide will be comprised of three main parts. When you thoroughly understand each part, and how to apply them in real life, doors will open. You'll soon see opportunities for these three various parts in all aspects of life. Even if you never get a job in sales, or never have to overly persuade anybody to do anything, the ideas in these three sections will make you a masterful communicator, easily able to shift people's emotions, covertly and elegantly, to wherever you'd like them to be.

Sales Structure

In this section, you'll learn the needed requirements of any sales situation. These elements must be present in any situation before a sales is made, even if one is buying from Amazon or any other Internet shop. You'll learn how to create these elements conversationally, and in what specific order. You'll learn how to test for each of the elements to make sure they are present before moving forward.

Conversational Hypnosis Structure

You'll learn the structure of conversational hypnosis. How it works and why. The necessary components. The gestures, how to choose the correct words using the correct tonality. How and when to pause. The secrets of easily bypassing the conscious critic that we all have.

The Structures

The structures themselves, those hypnotic scripts that you can memorize word for word, will be presented in three broad categories. Scripts to increase rapport. Scripts to increase buying desire. And scripts to increase feelings of financial abundance while simultaneously decreasing objections or obstacles. By doing these three things, and increasing the rapport your customers feel with you, their buying desire in your customers, and their general feeling of financial abundance while decreasing resistance, you will be able to sell many more things to a many more people.

How Long Will This Take?

It all depends on you. It's entirely possible to read through this entire guide, and gain an intellectual understanding in only a few hours. But it will take a lot longer to learn and memorize these structures so you can use them confidently with your customers. It also depends on what your sales experience is, and your level of self-confidence when using some of these "strange-sounding" techniques on strangers. If you have extensive experience and healthy confidence, the sooner you memorize a few of these structures, the sooner you'll start making more money. The structures themselves are 500-600 words apiece, and will take five minutes or so to execute conversationally. If learning these specific structures is all you need, then within a week you should have three or four memorized that you can try on your customers. If you are just starting out in sales, and this is the first book you've ever read, give yourself more time. But make no mistake – the simple ideas and techniques you learn in this guide are incredibly powerful. Consider making a strong choice - right here, right now - to do whatever it takes until you achieve full mastery of these techniques. Doing so will make you more attractive socially, and more successful financially.

Structures vs. Patterns

Often times you'll hear references to "language patterns," but in this guide, we will be using the word "structures." A language pattern is a sentence, and of little use on its own. These structures, as mentioned before, are several hundred words, and will be much more powerful. Think of a boxing metaphor. A language pattern is the equivalent of a single punch. A language structure is the equivalent of about three minutes of boxing. However, this is where the metaphor ends. You aren't going to beating anybody up, and the idea of "you vs. your customers" isn't appropriate.

Time Requirements

One of the significant differences between language patterns and language structures is their length. In the Milton Model, the base from which these structures are built, there are about fifty separate language patterns. That means there are millions of different potential combinations. Sure, you could take the time to learn them all individually, then practice various combinations on their own. But like learning how to box, that could take years. And I'm going to go out on a limb and guess that you don't want to wait for a year or two before you start making a lot of money. You want to start making it (or perhaps you *need* to) as soon as possible. And you absolutely can with these structures. But the trade-off to learning all of the individual patterns and the flexibility they will give you is time. This means they will only work if you have somebody's attention for five to ten minutes. If you had a year or two, you could learn the individual patterns, practice in them in back-and-forth conversations, and so on. Further, with the individual patterns, you literally can use them anywhere. Phone calls, emails, billboards. They can be the single punch that delivers the knock-out blow with surgical precision. For that reason, please consider taking the time to learn and study them. But to make money quickly, you'll need these structures. And these will only work in a one-on-one conversation (or sales presentation) with you doing most of the talking. These are not quick, magical one-liners that you can pull out any time. You'll need to set these up, and use two or three of these several hundred word structures within a conversation. For that reason, they are fairly restricted. Use them on the phone or face to face, but make sure they are done within an extended conversation.

That part is absolutely required. If you are cold-calling people, these won't be of much use. You'll need to be able to develop rapport, and elicit a few of their criteria. These are best used on warm customer who are expecting at least a ten minute conversation.

The good news is that if you have, or want to have, a sales job that requires face-to-face conversations for ten minutes or more, these patterns will work fantastically well. Sales will no longer be a guessing or a hoping game. After learning and trying out these structures and fine-tuning them to your own particular job, you'll create your own personal sales script that you can use over and over. Once you get to that level, that script will repeatedly get you sales. No more guesswork No more hoping. If you get consistent customers, you will get consistent sales, which translates to a consistent income.

1. The psychology of selling – attitude (How to connect to sales love and enjoy the process – to develop a theme)

➢ Once you've got a decent amount of rapport, and a good idea of their "surface-level" and "higher-level" criteria, you just keep expanding on that. Eliciting criteria and expanding criteria may be thought of in one step, but for the purposes of this guide, because there are several structures specifically to do this, it will be helpful to see them as separate. You can think of these two steps as mentally "asking what they want" and "taking what they want and blowing it up." Conversationally speaking, though, the uninitiated might not see a clear difference. As before, we'll look at three ways to do this: the "traditional" way, the "enlightened NLP" way, and the hypnotic way.

➢ Traditional Way

➢ This is the method of features and benefits. A customer walks into a shop and is greeted by a salesperson, who makes nice and finds out what the customer is looking for. He gets just enough criteria to find out they are looking for a microwave oven for their new apartment. He chooses one for the customer (or perhaps watches to see which direction they are looking in and selects the one with the highest price) and starts rattling off an endless list of features and benefits.

➤ This microwave has a 3,000-watt engine (or whatever they call them) and what that means is you can cook your frozen burritos in only seven seconds. Imagine how convenient that will be! No more wondering if you should stand there and stare at it for two minutes, or go back in front of the TV! With this baby, you stick it in, wait seven seconds and BOOM! A hot and juicy burrito with your name on it! You can even get up when the commercials start and be back when the show comes back on with a big plate of burritos and melted cheese, and a couple of beers! Imagine that!

➤ Now that was only one feature (a 3,000-watt element) and one benefit (fast cooking time). Suppose that salesperson had five or ten features and benefits, and each one was like the above paragraph. Now, that may be entertaining the shoppers who have time to kill, but what if the salesperson has bad breath or something? The idea behind this ubiquitous technique is that hopefully one or two of these feature-benefit combos will hit home, and the shopper will have his desire sufficiently increased. Needless to say, this process is hit or miss. Very little is known about the shoppers, so this ends up being a pure numbers game. The more people you spit out a bunch of features and benefits to, the more microwaves you'll sell.

➤ The Enlightened Approach

This is much better, but it can still use some improvement. This is when the enlightened salesperson actually asks the customer about all of the things they want to cook in their microwave. How often they'll use it. Whether or not it's going to be their "go-to" cooking tool in the kitchen. Armed with this information, it's a lot less pressure. This is a very straightforward approach. This is when you ask the customer what they want, and when you have enough detail, you show them that your product matches what they want. Why don't salespeople use this more often? Remember our discussion a couple of pages ago, how salespeople tend to enjoy persuading? That's one reason. Another reason is that salespeople believe that if they ask for too much criteria, it will be obvious that what they are shopping for is not available. Then what? Most salespeople would rather just get enough criteria to start and then turn around and bombard them with endless features and benefits. Also consider that when most people go shopping for things, even large possessions like houses or cars, they really don't have a concrete idea of what they want. If a salesperson asks for criteria, and they get a "Gee, I'd never really thought about it," the logical outcome would be the salesperson's worst nightmare: "I guess we need to go home and think about this."

➢ Hypnotically Expanding Desire

Even if they aren't sure what they want, this works great. All you need is to know that they want something similar to what you have to offer. Once you've got that, then you just keep expanding more and more, like we discussed in the last chapter. Let's say they are looking for a house, but they aren't sure what kind. Just ask them very vague questions about their ideal future with regards to a house. This doesn't even need to be related to the nitty-gritty details. So long as you are ready to set your anchors (the right hand whenever you repeat back their trance words or higher-order criteria), you'll be fine. So, assuming they are looking at a house, here are some possible questions, which can be used so long as they match the natural flow of the conversation:

➢ Do you like parties?

➢ What would be an ideal party in your house a year from now? Can you describe it?

➢ Are you hoping to start a family? Assuming everything goes perfectly, what would a typical Sunday morning be like in whatever house you decide to get, once the kids are up and walking on their own?

➢ What kind of hobbies do you enjoy? Can you imagine what it would be like, after having all your equipment moved in to your new house and getting into it every Saturday afternoon (or whenever they have time)?

➤ Imagine that this ends up being the perfect house. Imagine it's a year into the future, and you are reflecting on your decision to buy this particular home. Is there anything that happened that you wish you would have known about sooner?

➤ There really is no limit to these questions. And you really can't go on too long asking them, summarizing their answers (using their words and matching them to the right-side anchor). When people shop for anything expensive, they've got both worries and dreams. By putting these questions in "magical ideal future" perspective, they can temporarily forget about any potential issues and dream big. The more you get them dreaming big, and attaching the words they use to describe their dreams to your anchors, the better positioned you'll be. As you get into the later stages of the sale, you can drop in a couple of the story structures specifically designed to jack up their desires to wonderful levels of irresistibility.

2. Why you need techniques concluding sales?

Of course, if you talk to a customer about their dreams all day long, they'll love you (they may even invite you to dinner and introduce you to their daughter), but unless you ask them to buy something, all of their cash is going to stay safely in their wallets. And no matter how much you build up their massive desire, when you ask for the sale, they are going to ask how much. And unless you are working for an evil company that is secretly undercutting all the competition in its quest for world domination, they're going to look at the price and think, "Wow, that much, huh?" This is precisely why closing is the hardest part for most salespeople. And if you go into any high-end retail shop that pays good commissions, the "closers" are gods among men. Some shops even have only male closers. The regular salespeople "warm them up" and then the closer steps in. And in most processes, the act of lowering resistance is synonymous with closing. But it doesn't have to be. Think of closing as the very last step, the one that is automatic and so easy. It's just a matter of filling out that boring paperwork. And in order to do that, you've got to lower their resistance before they are even thinking about it. How will we do that? First, let's look at some typical ways of lowering resistance.

Features and Benefits

It's hoped that by building up enough desire with the features and benefits strategy, they'll be hooked to the product somehow. A common strategy that follows this is when the price is introduced, even if it's too high, the salesperson would say something like, "Well, I think my manager is a bit hung over today. Maybe I'll be able to talk him down. If I could get this for, say, 20% off, would we have a deal?" And the couple thinks for a minute and nods their heads hopefully. Then the salesperson disappears for a while. The idea is that while he's gone, the couple is looking at the product and slowly starting to convince themselves that if the salesperson can't get 20% off, they'll take it for 15% instead. Once they make that step, it "feels" like a commitment. At that point, they've more or less purchased it; they just don't know yet at what price. This, is more or less, the entire strategy behind those high sticker prices on cars.

Advanced Strategy

This is more or less the same strategy. It doesn't really lower resistance; rather, it builds up the desire significantly. And it does work. After all, to make a sale, the cost has to be perceived as less (subjective according to the buyer or actor) than the benefit. Of course, all else equal, we humans would rather get the same benefit for less cost, so there is always going to be a little bit of haggling. But building up desire to make the cost seem less by comparison is a common strategy among most sales professionals, enlightened or otherwise.

Hypnotic Lowering of Resistance

First, we'll outframe from cost to resistance. When selling anything, costs are associated with money. Once we start talking in terms of resistance, this is easier. At first, it may seem to make things more difficult. After all, buying a car slightly out of a person's price range is one thing. But buying an expensive car that their friends might not pprove of, or spending more time washing it, or more money on gas as their new SUV gets less mileage than their sedan) is something lse. So at first glance, talking about general resistance seems to be ;oing on the wrong direction. But in reality, resistance, in general, ompared to cost, is much easier for them to overcome on their own, s it's not usually defined very clearly.

How to Do

'he process is simple. The specific language will change from person o person, and product to product. The idea is to get them in the uture, after they've already made the decision to purchase the)roduct, and compare the things that would fall under the category of esistance from that perspective. Think about what this does. When)eople are shopping for something, both the pros and cons (criteria ind resistance) are vague. You first build up their criteria by talking ibout their ideal future. Things they can imagine, given a perfect)urchase. Then you put them in the future (which will be easy, as 'ou've already made it sufficiently bright for them) and, from that)erspective, get them to identify any items as resistance. This will ikely be the first time they think about these things. And they will be hinking about them, from an imaginary future, after envisioning an deal outcome to a potential purchase. All resistance looks huge if we ee it before we overcome it, but it looks tiny if we look at it after we've)vercome it. And this is what you are carefully doing. You are helping hem to imagine the resistance, for the first time, from the imaginary)erspective of their ideal future.

Potential Questions

Now, imagine having this for a year or two. And of course, it's not)erfect. There are some issues that have come up that you didn't inticipate. How do those look now, from this ideal future? Does it nake you question the purchase? Or is it something that is acceptable o you?

'hen you can go through and find several things to view from the ideal uture. This sounds goofy, and you may feel like they'll think you're rying to con them or something. But remember the sequence. You)uild rapport and use hypnotic stories to deepen it. You build their criteria, and then you use hypnotic stories to explode their desires You've created a very pleasant imagination for them. They will want t explore it in detail. And if you start to ask questions that purposel help them focus on potential problems in their future, what do yo think this will feel like from their perspective? You are not only helpin them create an ideal future, but by forcing them to imagine an potential drawbacks, you are going to be seen as someone actuall helping them ensure it's what they really want. What salesperson eve asks any question like, "Are you sure you really want this?" But ther you are, helping them come up with potential problems in their future

It Gets Better

Of course, you will be learning some very powerful hypnotic storie that lower their resistance, but in a very clever – and very POWERFU – way!

3. Steep chips (tricks) of the best sellers in the world - (examples)....
Summary of steps

Now we're ready to get to the stories. But before we do, let' summarize what we've covered so far. In the preceding chapters, we'v gone over the basic strategy, and we've left a few "placeholders" wher you can later insert the hypnotic stories. Then we'll go over th techniques used in the stories, and then we'll get to the storie themselves.

All Sales is Trade

All sales involve trading what the customer has (cash or futur payments) for what the customer wants (your product or service.) T the extent you can convince them that what you have is more valuabl to them, based on their own subjective viewpoint, you will get a sale commission, and eventually many more digits (on the left side of th decimal point) on your bank statement.

Rapport is King

If you only do one thing, build rapport. Tell all the relationship-building stories while matching their body language. The more rapport you build, the better you'll do. If you build this up enough, even if the guy or girl sitting in front of you doesn't buy anything, they'll spread the word to their friends. The only constraint you should worry about when building rapport is time – both yours and your customer's. But if you've got time, use it to build rapport.

Tell Hypnotic Rapport Stories

Mix in at least one story that is written to build rapport (worry about the details later). Mix this in and out of the natural rapport-building conversation as much as you can.

Elicit Criteria

Once you've got enough rapport, find out what they want. Get them in the mindset of, "Forgetting all about price, what would be the ideal situation with regards to this product or service?" Find out the bare-bones lower-order criteria (SUV or sedan, how many bedrooms, specific requirements for an investment plan, etc.) and start getting higher-order criteria. Why do they want an SUV instead of a sedan? Why four bedrooms and not five or three?

Expand Criteria

Once you've got a few layers of criteria, start talking in hypothetical land. Ask them to describe a few different ideal futures, assuming everything works out and they've got the perfect house, the perfect vehicle or the perfect retirement plan. Be sure to be constrained to reality; don't let them dream of a retirement plan that doubles every month, but let them fully imagine that all their needs are met, all of their anxieties are gone, and they can enjoy life to the fullest.

Anchor Trance Words

Whenever they are describing their ideal future, anchor it on the right side. Repeat back to them – do not paraphrase – using their exact words. Be sure to validate and honor what they are saying. Imagine that the more bright and concrete you can make their dreams, the more likely you will get paid. Leave your ideas about their dreams at home. As you repeat back their words, using them to describe their dreams, anchor the key points and phrases. Remember the key points and phrases as much as you can.

Hypnotically Expand Desire

Tell one or two hypnotic stories designed to expand desire. Weave these in and out of your conversation about their ideal future. Be careful not to "overwrite" their stories with your stories. They are telling you about their ideal future, and you are telling them stories that their ideal future brings to mind. These are carefully designed to make their ideal future seem much brighter and more compelling.

Future Pace

Ask them to look at the potential purchase from an imaginary point in the future after they've already made the purchase. Make sure they look at all potential issues from this angle.

Elicit Buying Strategy

Acknowledge that you understand price will be an issue. Ask them how they've made other purchases and get them to describe their buying strategy to you. Encourage them to talk about how they've thought rationally about buying products. Whenever they explain times when they've decided not to buy a product, nod your head and agree. Whenever they explain how they've decided to buy a product, nod your head and agree, repeat back their words, and set the "overcome objections" anchor. The more of these you set, the better off you'll be.

Tell Hypnotic Objection Stories

These are stories carefully written to pace them on a subconscious level as the characters in your stories overcome objections again and again. You'll also mix anchors. The anchor on the right-hand side means "something I really want" from your customer's perspective. These stories will slowly change into feelings of a positive financial future. These will build up their feelings of potential and their feelings of financial abundance in the near and long-term future. The main idea of these stories is to make them feel financially capable to easily make any purchase.

Closing

Ah, the scariest part! Lucky for you, it will be the easiest part. On your left side is the anchor that says, "Objections are nothing, I can demolish them with ease!" in your customer's mind. On your right side is the anchor that says, "I want this, and I want this right now!" combined with "I have a bright financial future!" Closing will be the simplest part.

"Well Mr. Customer, we've talked about all the things about this (right anchor) and how you might use this (right anchor) in the future. I think you'll agree that whenever you decide to get this (right anchor), it will be a wise decision. You also have a good idea of the price (left anchor) and I'll leave it up to you to decide if this item (right anchor) is worth this price (left anchor). What would you like to do (right anchor)?"

Hypnotic Story Structure

If this is your first experience with hypnotic stories, or "nested loops," as they are technically called, they will seem a bit goofy, and it will take some practice until you can deliver them with fluency. One of the reasons they are structured in the way they are is to bypass the "conscious critic." That's the part of our consciousness that is hypercritical of any questionable information, especially stuff we need to pay money for, or make any kind of commitment to. Think of it this way – if early humans were too easy to trick, we never would have survived as a species. We would have been conning each other so much that no one would have anything. But more importantly, women would always be tricked into sleeping with guys that weren't interested in sticking around. Whatever your thoughts are on religion or the role of the family in modern society, if our ancient cave-people ancestors were nothing more than players and single moms, we wouldn't have accomplished much. There was no government or welfare system to take care of people back then, so single moms and their kids would have starved to death. And it's a strange quirk of evolution that if any "thinking strategy" works for both men and women, then it's going to be included in both of our respective thinking patterns. And that, again, is our hypersensitivity to anybody that even sounds like they are up to no good. Therefore, metaphors rarely work if they are given in an "advice sounding" way. Anything that sounds like advice is going to trigger that conscious critic that is hypersensitive to anybody other than ourselves telling us what we should be doing.

Sales Example

Let's say you've got a customer warmed up to buy your product. You show them the price, and they clutch their chest in agony. Okay, maybe they don't do that, but you realize the deal has just vaporized before you, and that commission check you were counting before it hatched went right along with it. Let's say you pull out this crafty metaphor:

"Well, sure, it's expensive. But once upon a time in ancient Egypt, there was a guy who wanted to buy a camel, but he couldn't afford it. But when he realized how much value he could get out of the camel, he realized that this was a deal that he couldn't pass up, and he decided to buy it. And everybody lived happily ever after."

Your customer would see right through it! He'd look at you, smirk, and maybe say, "Seriously? A camel?" This is why you need to use some powerful storytelling technology to take that metaphorical guard of their brain (the conscious critic) and lull him or her peacefully to sleep. That's why any salesperson worth his salt always has a chloroform-soaked handkerchief in their back pocket. Just kidding. Don't do that – you'll end up in prison! But when you tell these stories in the right way, they will have that effect on their mind. They'll feel a comfortable numbness wash over their consciousness, as if they are back in elementary school, listening to story time at their local library.

Non-Linear Stories

Most stories are told linearly: beginning to middle to end. And because we tell stories in this way, we expect stories to always be told this way. This means if you happen to be telling a really boring story (which most people do unfortunately), they may pay attention to the beginning, but once it becomes clear how the story is going to end, they'll shut down their attention, but keep politely looking at you. If you tell linear stories in a sales situation, you might be thinking you are warming a customer up for your biggest commission ever, but they're busily planning what they are going to cook for dinner. So, instead, you tell the stories in a way that forces the customer to pay attention.

Broken Stories or Nested Loops

Let's say you've got a story that can be broken down into five chunks, or scenes. And let's say the third scene of each story is the high point, or the tension point. Once you get to part four, when the tension is starting to be resolved, people can see where the story is going, and that's when they start planning their dinner. But what happens when you tell several stories, and break each one off right when it's getting good?

Content is Gone - Emotions Remain

Most of the content, which is the actual thing the story is about, will be forgotten. Maybe the audience will remember stories one and two, but stories three and four (sandwiched in between one and two) will be forgotten. The emotions the story generated, however, will be remembered. And those emotions are going to be the ones that push them over the edge from being interested in the product, and deciding that they actually have to *have* the product. Because along with the stories, you are going to be using some very powerful hypnotic technology. That's what we'll cover next.

These are the techniques you'll be using within the stories. Don't worry – we won't go too much into details. Just enough so when you see these techniques in the stories themselves, you'll know what to do. These are things that are incredibly simple, but few people ever use them. This just means that when you use these techniques on your customers, they will likely have never seen them before. Once you get a feeling of how these work and how effective they are, you'll wonder why more people aren't using them. But remember, a few chapters ago, when we talked about how most sales people like the idea of overtly persuading someone? The biggest drawback to these techniques is accepting that no one will ever know you are using them. They will make you very persuasive. They will make you very wealthy. But that will only happen if you can get your ego out of the equation completely (at least long enough to get them to sign on the dotted line). This is much harder than you may realize. The desire for recognition is strong. When these work, the customer will actually believe that it was absolutely and completely their idea. They will never look at you and say, "Wow, you're an awesome salesperson. Thanks for showing me the light!" They will experience you as relaxed, pleasant and non-pushy (if not maybe a little long-winded), but they will not see you as a typical persuasive salesperson. This is precisely how these techniques worked when their inventor, Dr. Milton Erickson, used them. People would come to him with horrible emotional problems they'd had for years. He would start telling them goofy and confusing stories. They would leave, thinking, "Dude, what the heck was that all about?" But their problems would be gone. Poof. Your customers will be the same. What problems do they have that you will poof into nothingness? Any resistance to buying your product. They'll have a memory of your just showing them the product and explaining it a little bit, but they'll imagine it was they who thought about it and made the buying decision. The only thing standing between you and big fat commission checks (besides doing your due diligence to learn these story structures effectively) is your ego. If you need to be recognized for your persuasive superpowers, you'll need to do some work. But don't worry – it seems that the natural arch-enemy to your ego, that part of you that craves recognition, is a big fat commission check. You just need to turn off your desire for recognition long enough to get paid. Then you can take your paycheck, go to your favorite bar and buy a round for everyone. OK, enough long winded warnings. Let's get to the nuts and bolts.

Pauses

Most people pause where they would normally put a period in a sentence. For example, they would say:

"Yesterday I went to the store. (pause) When I got there I bought a banana. (pause) Then I went outside and ate the banana. (pause) It was pretty fun."

Say that out loud. It sounds normal. Not interesting (unless you love stories about bananas). Now say the exact same thing, but with the pauses shuffled around a bit.

"Yesterday I went to the (pause) store. When I got there, I bought a (pause) banana. Then I went outside and (pause) ate the banana."

Say that out loud, and specifically don't pause unless it says pause. For some reason, we humans have a hard time not focusing intently when someone uses pauses in this manner. This is fun to try with a group of friends, and when you get to the pauses, slowly look around before you continue. Even if you are telling a normal story about a normal guy eating a normal banana, people will find something very funny about the situation.

Anchors

We've already talked about these. For the sake of this course, we'll use (R) to refer to an anchor on the right side of your body, and (L) for the left side. You "set" these anchors when you repeat something back. For example, when you've heard some particularly juicy trance words, repeat them back and simply gesture on your right side, like people normally do, when you say the words. People gesture all the time, but never consciously, so it will feel a bit weird. It will get easier with practice. And when you "set" the (L) gesture, remember, it's about their telling you how they decided to buy something in the past. And when you repeat the specific reason they decided to buy something, or any other "trance words" that seem more important than their other words when describing their previous purchases, "set" the left anchor by gesturing to the left. You will "fire" the anchors, meaning when you use them later, after you've set them, they will recall a portion of those same feelings they experienced when you set them. The more you set, the better, and the more you fire, the better. Just be sure to be consistent. Only use gestures when setting and firing these specific anchors. This will take time, but it will be worthwhile. It will also give you a kind of X-ray vision when watching people speak, especially politicians. Despite many beliefs to the contrary, most politicians are not trained in NLP (Neuro-linguistic programming) in any way. This will be clear next time you see a politician speaking, and find it nearly impossible to find any correlation their gestures and the meaning (right, wrong, desires, etc.) in the various portions of their message.

Self-Point

This is a very good anchor to use whenever possible, regardless of whether you are selling something or having an easygoing conversation with your life partner. This is when you casually refer or gesture toward yourself when you say anything that will be accepted as something "good." Or you can use this interchangeably with the right-side anchor (the thing they want in their ideal future). You just bring one or both hands briefly towards yourself, just like a regular gesture. Something like the following would be perfect:

"Last week I was watching the news and they said the economy is expected to do really well (SP) in the next couple of years. Then I was flipping around and they had this goofy game show, and this really nice (SP) old woman, they said she was a librarian or something, won a million dollars (SP) by answering some weird question about ancient ninja history or something. Later they asked how she knew that – it had something to do with comic books and how she was always reading comic books about superheroes (SP) in the library where she works. That's pretty cool (SP), isn't it?"

Now, just for the sake of demonstration, practice saying that out loud, in the mirror, while practicing the self-points (SP), but with these strategically placed pauses (P):

"Last week I was watching the (P) news and they said the economy is expected to do really (P) well (SP) in the next couple of years. Then I was flipping around and they had this goofy (P) game show, and this

22

really nice (SP) old woman, they said she was a (P) librarian or something, won a million dollars (SP) by answering some weird question about ancient (P) ninja history or something. Later they asked how she knew that – it had something to do with (P) comic books and how she was always reading comic books about (P) superheroes (SP) in the library where she works. That's pretty cool (SP), isn't it?"

There is one more powerful piece of hypnotic technology that gets a chapter all to itself. The most famous and, fortunately (for you!), misused piece of technology from NLP and Covert Hypnosis...the famous embedded command, coming next!

Embedded Commands

These are, at the same time, the most widely known technique from NLP and (luckily) the most misunderstood and improperly used. Why would this be a good thing? Because most goofs who use these don't really have any idea what they are doing, they will be ineffective. But when you learn how to use them correctly, they will have a profound effect. And you will be using commands much more effectively than even many NLP instructors. Let's get to it.

What's a Command?

Do this! Commands are simple verb-object or verb-phrase combinations in the imperative form. Don't worry about the grammar; it's just a command. An order. Not a request, not a suggestion – a command. How do you say a command? With a slightly downward tone at the end. Say "Sit down" as flatly as you can. You'll likely sound like a bored teacher waiting for the kids to finish whatever they are doing before they finally decide to sit. Now say "Sit down" with a slight downward tone at the end. It sounds more authoritative. But don't go too far. Now say "Sit down" as if your head would explode if they didn't immediately obey. You want to be just slightly authoritative, but not too much. The whole point of "embedded" commands is you're supposed to "hide them" in a sentence. Remember, when you are using these, they are within nested stories specifically designed to fade their minds a bit while they lazily follow your words. If you say the commands so they sound too different from the rest of the words, it will break the trance and you'll lose everything you've gained. If you say them too lightly, they won't have much of an effect. How lightly? Just barely is enough. Remember, you'll also be using these commands along with those gestures, so you won't really need to say them much differently than you normally do. Milton Erickson, the Physician-Hypnotist whose invention (Ericksonian Hypnosis) this is modeled after, would only tilt his head slightly when he said his embedded commands. He didn't use gestures because his subject's eyes were usually closed; all he had to do to "mark off" the commands was say them from a slightly different physical location (tilted head vs. non-tilted head).

How to Embed Them

To embed a command, just put the imperative inside a larger sentence. If the command is "Sit down," then it can be embedded inside the following sentence:

"Sometimes people like to **sit down** when they listen to this, as it helps them to **relax** easily."

Here you have two commands, "sit down," later followed by "relax." The general rules when embedding is that shorter is better than longer, and the middle of a sentence (or separate from any pauses) is better than the end. For example,

"Some people like to **sit down** when they listen."

is better than

"A lot of people like to **sit down**. (P) What would you like?"

and

"A lot of people like to **sit down** while they listen."

is better than

A lot of people like to **sit down in a chair** while they listen."

Both "Sit down" and "Sit down in a chair" are commands, but the first is much easier for a partially hypnotized mind to wrap itself around. Remember, the whole idea is to make it as easy and comfortable as possible for your customers to follow along with your suggestions. If you rattle off a five- or six-word embedded command while gesturing like a madman, they are going to know something's up. But if you say a simple two-word command, along with a very brief right-side gesture, and just keep talking as if nothing happened, it will slip right past their barely awake conscious critic and straight into their unconscious.

Stacking Commands

When people hear about commands, they feel as if they've discovered the secret alchemy of the human mind. And in a way, they have. However, they aren't silver bullets. They are very powerful as long as you use them the right way in the right context, and in the right order. The most famous embedded command is "buy now," which is supposed to be used wherever you'd say "by now." For example, if you look at your customer and say,

"Well, **by now,** Mr. Customer, I've explained all the details so **by now** you probably have an idea of whether or not you want to **get this now** or think about it for a couple days."

If you wait until the last possible moment to use these, they won't have much of an effect. But if you use many of them, and put them in the right order, they will have a much more powerful effect. Think of embedded commands like bees. Probably not the best metaphor, as you want to help your customers and not sting them to death, but the bee metaphor will help you remember the necessity of using as many commands as you can. If you found one bee in your house, you'd squish it and then forget about it. But if you found a swarm or a hive in your wall, you wouldn't be able to sleep until an exterminator came and took care of them. Think of embedded commands as your personal swarm of bees destroying all the resistance in the mind of your customer, so they can enjoy the sweet honey of your product or service (yeah, terrible, I know!).

When you are using several commands in a row, start with simple ones, and then slowly build up to the more difficult ones. For example commands like "Enjoy life" or "Make money" or "Have lots of sex" or "Become popular" are things that most normal people will want to do anyway. And by putting them in command form, you'll warm them up to the structure. Then you can slip in some neutral commands like "Open up" or "Think about this" or "Consider this" or "Imagine you future." Once you've got a few of those out of the way, you can drop in the heavy hitters like "Buy now" or "Make a decision" or "Take this home" or "Give me all your money," among others.

Now that we've got all the nuts and bolts in place, we're ready for the patterns themselves.

4. Types of customers. (Write several different types of customers)

As a salesperson, your customer and his needs should be your first priority. Always cater to this before all else. Humans are not machines so, more often than not, most of the customers will buy your products because they like you rather than for pricing or any other objections. A salesman-customer relationship needs as much sensitivity in handling as any other personal relationship.

A few positive attitudes that will endear you to your customers:

- Friendliness
- Charm
- Honesty and candor

The last point is applicable both to you as a person and to your products. Never try to cover up a product's defects. Present it differently, perhaps, or be up-front and tell them there is a problem always including a solution for the problem in your sales pitch.

Listen to your customers – only when you listen to your customer, can you realize what his actual needs are. Asking what he wants and then delivering his needs in a neat package will make him your customer for life.

And do not merely listen to him. Integrate the words you are hearing with his non-verbal gestures and clearly understand what he is trying to communicate. For example, he may be rattling off his needs in terms of technical details, but if he appears jumpy and worried, remember not to add to his worry with your long-drawn, time-consuming sales pitch. Give him a crisp, immediate solution that will ease his concerns.

Give your customer your full attention. Ensure mobile devices are off or on silent during your meeting. Allow nothing to disturb your focus from your customer. When interacting with your customer, he must feel that you are there only for him and all other priorities have been shelved for his sake.

However, once you have given him what he wants, allow him breathing space. It would be quite annoying to cling to him until the deal is actually through. This kind of confidence will come when you have managed to sell him your product so well that he will not want to look at any other competitor.

Use demonstrative and illustrative examples. Getting a reluctant customer to buy your product requires more than flowery, fanciful language and your articulation abilities. When this fails, illustrate or show him what your product does. If it is a financial product, show him an Excel sheet with the amount that he will have at the end of the transaction. If it's a consumer good, demonstrate its operation.

If it is solar panels, show him the savings on electricity bills. If it is chocolate, give him a taste of it. If it is a guitar, let him play it. Remember to talk about the benefit of the product rather than the product itself. Focus on what the product does instead of getting into descriptive details.

Customer is king in the marketplace and you have to keep them happy. Here are a few reasons to explain why you must endeavor to keep your customers happy and satisfied:

- "No customers" translates to "no business." There are no businesses in the world that thrive or even exist in the absence of customers. Mahatma Gandhi once said to a banking employee complaining about unrelenting customers, "A customer is the most important visitor to your premises." This is absolutely true and you must give customers the respect they deserve for being the most important set of stakeholders in your business.

- How a customer sees your product determines whether your sale is a success or not. There are times when the customer might see an imperfect aspect of your product. Despite his seemingly erroneous perception, he will buy the product because he sees it that way. It would be quite futile for you to change his perception unless, of course, the way he sees it is not getting you the sale! Then, you need to work on getting him to change his perception. Whatever it is, the product is bought because the customer sees it in a particular way!

- It is far easier to keep existing customers happy rather than hunt for and gather new ones. Both cost-wise and effort-wise, this aspect is true. Keeping existing customers also has a second benefit: they will advertise your product by word of mouth and at no extra cost to you!

- Unhappy customers can turn into your biggest foe. Just as happy customers can advertise your product, unhappy customers can ruin your reputation through word of mouth. Keeping customers happy is, therefore, critical to your sales success.

To summarize, "customer is king" is an old yet timeless adage that will not go out of fashion. It is thus your duty to give him your best, be aware of his power, refrain from having a condescending attitude toward him, make things easy for him, and allow him to call the shots.

Of course, all this does not mean you allow him to override and bulldoze you in every way. It simply means packaging the product the way the customer wants it. Ensure that he feels happy with what he has received. This will make him your loyal client.

Treating your customers with respect and dignity is the first step towards making a good salesperson and increasing your sales numbers. No matter which industry you work in, existing and potential customers are your most valuable assets and how they perceive you will decide how well your sales career is moving.

5. Gathering information about the client. How can we unravel the true interests of the client (asking the right questions)

Just as we are developing the ways that we interact and develop relationships with our customers, so too are they developing the way that they make decisions about how and why they purchase. These decision-making processes are constantly changing, so it is important to continually re-evaluate the way that you go about selling your products and services to your customers. You must also remember the difference between sales and marketing, and make sure that when you are selling, you do not come across as arrogant or not paying attention to what the customer has said in relation to what they actually need from you.

In essence, a sales strategy consists of a plan that positions a company's brand or product in order to gain a competitive advantage. The most successful types of sales strategies assist your sales team in focusing on target market customers and communicating with them in helpful, relevant and meaningful ways. Your sales representatives – and you – need to know how your products and/or services can be used to solve your customers' problems. To be successful, your sales strategy should always be focused on presenting to the customers within your target market; otherwise, you will be wasting time trying to sell to customers for whom you have not tailored your products.

In saying this, you should be well aware by now that in the sales business, your customer's needs should always come first. You should be asking as many relevant and quality questions as possible to ensure that what you are offering your customer is actually what they need. Sales is built on trust, and repeat business is the foundation of long-term success in the sales industry (or any business, for that matter), so let's have a look at six of the most effective steps that you can implement today to help you make sales and close the deal more efficiently.

IDENTIFY WHO MAKES THE BUYING DECISIONS

When selling, it is quite obvious that the only person who will buy or has the authority to buy is the decision-maker. This especially applies when you are trying to win over the business of a new customer. You should always do your research first and try and understand how the decision-maker makes decisions, what motivates them to buy, and so on. Always customize and personalize your sales pitch so that you are specifically targeting that customer, and only that customer, at that time.

BE REALISTIC

When tailoring your sales pitch for the customer, make sure that you do not come across as too calculated, as this can actually scare some people off. In other words, show the customer that you care about identifying their needs and providing a solution to fix those needs rather than just making a quick sale. Remember that honesty and relationship-building are keys to success in the sales industry.

CREATE URGENCY

Your goal, as a successful salesperson, is to get the customer to buy right now. You can't let your customer walk out of the door and say that they will be back next week, because they will either never come back, or will buy from someone else (your competition!). Whether you use your skills of persuasion by asking questions, offer a discount if they purchase right now, or simply inform them that this price is only valid for today – when they come back next week, the product will be more expensive.

DEALING WITH OBJECTIONS

As discussed in Chapter Two, we need to ask for the sale in a way that if the customer is going to say no, they are obligated to say more than no. Remember, "If I gave you the product at this low price, would there be any reason you would not want to buy it today?" This sentence should be used at the end of every single one of your sales pitches. Not every customer, no matter how hard we try, is going to buy from us. But, we need to make sure that we understand and ask the reasons for their not buying with us. If we start to notice a pattern with customers who are not buying for similar reasons, we may need to change the way that we are dealing with things.

KNOW WHO YOUR COMPETITORS ARE

Running a business is tough. Consumers these days have so much variety in product and price that you really need to stand out if they are going to buy from you. Look what your competition is doing, and then aim to constantly do better. You may not be able to always beat their prices, but you can definitely offer a higher quality of customer service – after all, sales businesses are built on relationships and repeat business.

BE PROFESSIONAL AT ALL TIMES

If your customer asks you a question that stumps you during your sales pitch, never make something up just to keep the pitch flowing. Tell your customer that you do not know, but you will find out the answer for them. You do not want to be caught delivering false promises. Only talk about what you know, and maintain a high level of respect and professionalism with all of your customers at all times.

6. Non-verbal communication in the work of the seller with the client. Component of nonverbal communication (space, facial expressions, gaze, intonation, body movement).

In order to be successful in sales, you must learn how to be a great leader. Anyone can be a leader, but true leadership comes from the deep innate ability or skill that allows you to influence people. If you look back through the pages of history, strong and influential people have ruled armies, which had built dynasties and toppled kingdoms although our sales business should not be managed to that extreme. The first step that you should take is to believe in yourself.

The biggest obstacle in doing this is that we as humans have the uncanny ability to constantly doubt ourselves. Thinking that we do not have what it takes to be the best that we want to be, we give in to fear and hinder our abilities before we even start. Realize that our biggest enemies are ourselves.

However, the most successful people that we see around us do not give in to this state of mind. They apply the five traits of successful people and overcome this silly obstacle, and then they are able to continue working on developing the skills required to influence people. The question is, how do we influence people? When you think about it, it really comes down to leading by example – that kind of leadership that you share with your closest friends and family members. So, the question should rather be, how do you make more friends?

Making more friends definitely sounds better than the phrase "winning" more friends. So, how can this be achieved? What is it that we do that makes friends for us? It really comes down to five skills which we should apply to every conversation that we have with people from sales prospects to strangers on the street.

1. Give your complete attention to someone else and show genuine interest in everything that they say to you.
2. Make sure that you do not forget their name (write it down if possible, or get a business card).
3. Listen to every word that they say.

4. Make the person feel important – that they are the center of your attention.
5. Smile and thank them for their time.

When you think about it, isn't this the way that we act around our close friends and family members? This is how you should be acting around every person that you meet. Remember that the secret to a successful sales business is to build relationships to form long-term customers who will buy from you many times, so if we are able to master the art of relationship building, we should be able to turn every person that we meet into a loyal customer for life.

7. Technique of "Mirroring" as an effective management technique the process of the transaction.

Did you make a choice? I chose the previous letters because they're commonly used as the first letter in people's names (e.g., Joe, Meghan, Lauren, Kevin). If the first letter of your name appears in that list, you were more likely to choose that letter.

This chapter will explain why that occurs and why we non-consciously gravitate toward things that we perceive to be similar to us. As you'll learn in this chapter, revealing nearly any form of similarity – no matter how small or insignificant it may appear – can tremendously boost your persuasion.

THE POWER OF SIMILARITIES

If you're reading this book, then you probably find psychology interesting. What a coincidence . . . I love psychology too!
One of the most powerful factors that can influence your chances of gaining compliance is the amount of rapport that exists between you and your target. The more he likes you, the greater your chances of succeeding; the less he likes you, the lower your chances. Although the title of this chapter could have been "Build Greater Rapport," the topic of building rapport is extremely broad, so this chapter focuses on explaining the single most effective strategy: emphasizing similarities that you share with your target (for a more comprehensive explanation

of rapport-building techniques, refer to Dale Carnegie's classic book, *How to Win Friends and Influence People*).

The old saying "Opposites attract" is almost entirely wrong. Extensive research shows that we're psychologically drawn toward people who resemble ourselves in appearance, interests and virtually all other aspects. The principle of incidental similarity explains how rapport can develop when two people discover a shared similarity, even a small and irrelevant similarity, such as a shared love for psychology (wink wink).

Our psychological compulsion to gravitate toward similarities is so powerful that it can even dictate our lives. How so? In a fascinating study, Pelham, Mirenberg and Jones (2002) found some peculiar surprises:

- People named Dennis are disproportionately more likely to become dentists, and people named George or Geoffrey are disproportionately more likely to work in fields of the geosciences (e.g., geology).

- Roofers are 70 percent more likely to have names beginning with the letter R, and hardware store owners are 80 percent more likely to have names beginning with the letter H.

- People named Philip, Jack, Mildred and Virginia are more likely to reside in Philadelphia, Jacksonville, Milwaukee and Virginia Beach, respectively.

Needless to say, similarities are another powerful force that non-consciously guide our behavior.

As you'll learn in the rest of this chapter, this principle extends beyond mere letters. You'll learn why nearly any form of similarity that you share with your target can help you build rapport and increase your chances of gaining compliance.

WHY ARE SIMILARITIES SO POWERFUL?

What make similarities so powerful? This section will describe two explanations that research has offered.

Evolution. The first explanation is evolution (Lakin et al., 2003). From an evolutionary perspective, our ancestors were drawn toward others who appeared similar because they seemed less threatening; if someone appeared dissimilar, they needed to exert more caution because they posed a greater threat. People who failed to exert more caution were often killed, and so those types of people were gradually wiped away over time. Because our ancestors were smart enough to realize the importance of similarities, they lived to pass on their adaptive traits, which is why similarities continue to exert tremendous power over us, even today.

Implicit Egotism. Although evolution is one explanation, the explanation that has garnered the most support is implicit egotism, a concept suggesting that we all possess an underlying sense of self-centeredness (Pelham, Carvallo, & Jones, 2005).

Due to our egotistical nature, we possess a hidden psychological urge to gravitate toward things that resemble us in any way. People named Dennis are more likely to become dentists because they have developed an affinity toward the letters in their name, and that affinity has guided their behavior toward an occupation containing the same letters from their name (Nuttin, 1985).

It might sound ludicrous, but there's ample evidence that shows our profound affinity toward the letters in our name, a concept known as the name-letter effect. Research shows that consumers significantly prefer brand names containing the same letters in their name (Brendl, et al., 2005), and this effect is so strong that those brands influence how people consume those products. For example, one study found that people named Jonathan will consume more of a Japanese drink called "Joitoki" (Holland et al., 2009).

Even beyond the name-letter effect, more support for implicit egotism can be found in our failure to recognize our own face. Imagine that someone took a picture of you and manipulated it to make new versions of that picture. Some pictures made you look more attractive, whereas other pictures made you look less attractive. If you were then presented with a line-up of your attractive and unattractive distortions, would you be able to recognize your actual picture? Of course, right? Well, it turns out that it might be harder than you think.

When researchers presented people with a line-up of attractive and unattractive distortions of their face, and when people were asked to choose their own true face, people consistently chose an attractive distortion of their face, rather than their own true face (Epley & Whitchurch, 2008). Our implicit egotism is so strong that we don't even recognize our own face!

PERSUASION STRATEGY: REVEAL ANY SIMILARITIES

Now that you understand why we gravitate toward similarities, this section will teach you how to use that knowledge to increase your chances of gaining compliance.

Incidental Similarity. Because we're psychologically compelled to gravitate toward similar stimuli, you can use this pressure to guide your target toward your intended goal by emphasizing any type of similarity that you share with your target. This incidental similarity will help you appeal to his implicit egotism, while building greater rapport and increasing your chances of securing his compliance.

To examine the impact of revealing any similarity, Jerry Burger and his colleagues (2004) told people that they were conducting an experiment on astrology. During the astrology-related tasks, participants discovered that they shared the same birthday with a fellow participant (who was actually a confederate working with the researchers). The researchers wanted to see if that incidental similarity would make that person more likely to comply with a request from the confederate.

When people believed that the experiment was finished, they left the room with the confederate and walked down the hall together. While walking, the female confederate asked the participant if he would help her with her English assignment. What was the assignment? She needed to find a student who would review her eight-page essay and write a one-page critique of her arguments (very far from an enticing request). However, the researchers found that people who discovered that they shared the same birthday with the confederate were significantly more likely to help with that demanding request.

After receiving those startling results, the researchers conducted a follow-up study to understand how the perceived rarity of a similarity fits into the equation. If we discover that we share a similarity with someone, does our propensity to help increase if that similarity is more uncommon?

The researchers examined that question by conducting the same experiment with new participants. This time, however, rather than discovering a shared birthday, participants discovered that they shared a similar fingerprint with the confederate. Some participants were told that the category of that fingerprint was common, whereas other participants were told that the category of the fingerprint was rare.

As expected, the percentage of compliance with the English assignment increased according to the rareness of the fingerprint.

- When people remained unaware that they shared a similar fingerprint, the percentage of compliance was 48 percent.

- When people discovered that they shared a similar yet common fingerprint, the percentage of compliance rose to 55 percent.

- When people discovered that they shared a similar and rare fingerprint, the percentage of compliance rose dramatically to 82 percent.

Although any similarity will make your target more likely to comply with a request, that pressure increases in accordance with the rarity of that similarity. But you should also keep in mind that the similarity doesn't need to be relevant or important, only uncommon (e.g., a rare fingerprint).

How can you apply that principle? If you're meeting your target for the first time, take a moment to learn about her: ask about her life, her interests and anything else. Not only does this action show interest (another technique to build rapport), but more importantly, it allows you to pinpoint similarities that you might share with your target.

Upon discovering a similarity, don't hesitate to reveal it so that you can appeal to her implicit egotism, especially if that similarity is uncommon. Even if the similarities seem irrelevant or unimportant (e.g., a shared first name, mutual friend, similar interest, etc.), those incidental similarities can dramatically boost your persuasion.

You could even use incidental similarity in conjunction with social norms. In one interesting study, Goldstein, Cialdini, and Griskeviciu (2008) examined how different messages would encourage hotel guests to reuse their towels. Take a guess which message had the greatest impact:

> HELP SAVE THE ENVIRONMENT. The environment deserves our respect. You can show your respect for nature and help save the environment by reusing your towels during your stay.

> JOIN YOUR FELLOW GUESTS IN HELPING TO SAVE THE ENVIRONMENT. In a study conducted in Fall 2003, 75% of the guests participated in our new resource savings program by using their towels more than once.

I'm sure you can guess by now that the second message elicited more compliance because it pointed the norm in the desired direction. And that's exactly what happened. The first message had a compliance rate of 37 percent, whereas the second message had a compliance rate of 44 percent.

But something interesting happened when the researchers tweaked the second message to emphasize a more uncommon similarity:

• JOIN YOUR FELLOW GUESTS IN HELPING TO SAVE THE ENVIRONMENT. In a study conducted in Fall 2003, 75% of the guests who stayed in this room participated in our new resource savings program by using their towels more than once.

When the researchers described that guests from the same room had reused their towel (a stronger similarity than simply staying at the same hotel), compliance jumped even higher to 49 percent. Why was that small change so profound? The next section will explain why belonging to a perceived "ingroup" can trigger a higher rate of compliance.

Ingroup Favoritism. A second application of similarities can be found in ingroup favoritism, the tendency for people to prefer groups that share a similar characteristic to themselves. Whether you attend the same school, play on the same sports team, or share the same hotel room, research shows that people generally prefer (and are more persuaded by) members of ingroups. In fact, when we merely view faces of people from an ingroup, there's greater neural activity in our orbito-frontal cortex, the brain region associated with rewards (Van Bavel, Packer, & Cunningham, 2008).

Research shows that we're easily persuaded by members of ingroups and easily dissuaded by members of outgroups. Consider a fascinating experiment. Imagine that you and a stranger are participating in a taste test, and both of you are allowed to take as much food as you want. The stranger takes a certain amount of food and walks away, and you're left standing in front of the food, contemplating how much to take. Researchers found that the amount of food you take would be greatly influenced by the characteristics of the other person and how much food she took (McFerran et al., 2010b).

In that study, the stranger was actually a thin female confederate. In some trials, she was her normal thin self, but in other trials, she wore a professionally-designed prosthesis (a suit that made her look overweight). The researchers wanted to examine how her body type – thin vs. overweight – would influence people's decision about how much food to take, and the results were startling.

The researchers found that people matched the confederate's portion size when she seemed thin, yet they took the opposite portion size when she seemed overweight. When the confederate was thin and took a small portion, people also took a small portion; when she took a large portion, people also took a large portion. But when the confederate appeared overweight, people chose the opposite portion size. When the confederate seemed overweight and took a large portion, people took a small portion; when she took a small portion, people took a large portion.

What sparked those results? When people appear overweight, they're perceived to be part of a dissociative group, a group from which other people try to "dissociate." People in the previous study took the opposite portion size when they perceived the confederate to be overweight because they felt a non-conscious pressure to distance themselves from her.

But here's a question: What if people in the previous study were on a strict diet? Wouldn't dieters identify with someone overweight because they both share a desire to lose weight? If that were the case, wouldn't the results flip because that similarity would make the confederate part of their ingroup? A second study examined whether that outcome occurs and it turns out...it does.

In a separate study that used a similar methodology, strict dieters identified with the confederate when she seemed overweight, whereas non-dieters identified more with the confederate when she was thin (McFerran et al., 2010a). In both cases, the dieters and non-dieters showed the greatest amount of persuasion (i.e., chose similar portion sizes) when they could identify with the confederate.

When trying to persuade someone, how can you demonstrate that you belong to the same ingroup? Not only can you use the first technique of revealing any type of similarity, but you can also simply use words like "we" and "us" to reinforce that you belong to the same ingroup. Research shows that these pronouns can trigger a feeling of pleasure because they convey that you belong to the same ingroup (Perdue et al., 1990).

When I was editing this book, I realized that I was explaining many of the psychological principles using third person examples (e.g., "people experience implicit egotism"), so I went through and changed all of the wording to first person examples (e.g., "we experience implicit egotism"). Did it help create rapport between me and you? Who knows? But it definitely didn't hurt.

Chameleon Effect. Here's a quick exercise you can try (but you should read this entire paragraph first so that you know what to do, then try the exercise). Hold your arms straight out in front of you, parallel to the floor, with your palms facing each other. Put about 3–5 inches of space between your palms, and then close your eyes. Once your eyes are closed, imagine that I placed two powerful magnets on the insides of both your palms, and then imagine that those magnets are pulling your hands together. Use all of your imaginative power to really feel those magnets pulling your hands closer toward each other. Do you understand what you're supposed to do? Great. Put the book down and do that exercise for about 30 seconds, and then come back here (by the way, if you skip ahead and read why I'm having you do this exercise, it won't have the same effect if you want to return to try it).

So, did you do the exercise? Welcome back. I'm sure that some of you were pretty startled when you felt your hands actually press together. I'm also sure that some of you opened your eyes after a minute with no change in your hand position whatsoever, only a heightened skepticism of this supposed "psychology." And I'm also sure that most of you kept reading without the slightest inclination to try the exercise because you're too resilient to take instructions from a mere book. Well played, my friend.

In any case, whenever I hypnotize someone, I use that exercise to test that person's level of hypnotizability. Though the test is by no means definitive, people who are hypnotizable generally show greater movement in their hands because their imagination causes their hands to move together more easily than those who are not as easily hypnotized.

The underlying principle behind that phenomenon is known as the ideomotor response, and it's our tendency to perform behavior upon merely thinking about that behavior. People who are more easily affected by the ideomotor response will exhibit greater movement in their hands when they simply imagine their hands moving closer together. But the ideomotor response also applies to areas beyond mere body movements. For example, thinking about aggression can trigger aggressive behavior (much like priming), which is one of the key reasons why violence in video games and movies can increase aggressive behavior in children (Anderson & Bushman, 2001).

How does this principle relate to similarities? When we speak with people, we examine their nonverbal behavior and experience a hidden psychological urge to mimic that behavior. If someone is speaking with his arms crossed, you may soon find yourself with your own arms crossed. If that person is speaking with an enthusiastic tone, you may find yourself using a similar upbeat tone.

Though it occurs outside of our conscious awareness, this chameleon effect is a key element in building rapport (Lakin et al., 2003). Not only do we tend to mimic people we like, but we also like people more when they mirror our own nonverbal behavior. In fact, researchers found the following outcomes when people imitated nonverbal behavior:

- Waitresses gained higher tips (Van Baaren et al., 2003).
- Sales clerks achieved higher sales and more positive evaluations (Jacob et al., 2011).
- More students agreed to write an essay for another student (Guéguen, Martin, & Meineri, 2011).
- Men evaluated women more favorably in speed dating (Guéguen, 2009).

Thus, not only do "incidental similarities" result in a greater likelihood to comply with a request, but so too does similar nonverbal behavior.

In addition to evolution and implicit egotism (the two reasons that were described earlier in the chapter), another reason why similar nonverbal behavior is so powerful can be found in our brain's desire for symmetry. When another person imitates our nonverbal behavior, this symmetry activates the medial orbitofrontal cortex and the ventromedial prefrontal cortex, brain regions that are associated with reward processing (Kühn et al., 2010). Mimicking behavior is so powerful because, in a way, the symmetry is biologically pleasing.

There are two basic strategies you can use to take advantage of this principle. The first should be pretty obvious: to gain compliance, you should build greater rapport by mimicking your target's nonverbal behavior. Commonly used by therapists to convey empathy (Catherall, 2004), this strategy has been implemented in various settings with remarkable success (as you can see in the previous list of experimental outcomes).

Due to the powerful impact of mimicking nonverbal behavior, you should always strive to make your request in person. Although that advice may sound somewhat foreign due to our technology- and e-mail-obsessed society, you're more likely to gain compliance when you make a request in person (Drolet & Morris, 2000). If your situation isn't conducive to an in-person interaction (e.g., far distance), you should use video conferencing or, at the very least, a phone call. The more nonverbal cues that are available, the more easily you can mimic them to build rapport with your target, which will increase your chances of gaining compliance.

To understand the second strategy of mimicry, think back to the concept of congruent attitudes and how we infer our attitudes by observing our body language and behavior. Remarkably, research reveals that we sometimes infer our attitudes by observing the behavior of others whom we perceive to be similar to us. Using an EEG (a brainwave recording device), Noah Goldstein and Robert Cialdini (2007) led people to believe that they shared similar brainwave patterns with a student who appeared in a video interview, which depicted the student's altruistic efforts toward helping the homeless. When the researchers asked participants to complete a questionnaire after watching the interview, people who were informed of the similar EEG patterns not only rated themselves to be more self-sacrificing and sensitive, but also significantly more likely to help the researchers in an additional study. People were more likely to assist in the additional study because they observed the altruistic behavior from the supposedly similar student, and they developed a congruent attitude from that student's behavior.

If your target perceives you to be similar, she will develop attitudes that are congruent with your behavior. Therefore, if your target perceives you to be similar, you should display behavior that's consistent with the attitude that you're trying to extract from your target. For instance, if one of your close friends is starting to struggle in school, you should make an effort to have occasional study sessions together, even if you're not in the same class. The simple exposure to seeing you study might help your friend develop a genuine interest in studying more, which could help boost her grades. Even if you simply talk about your interest in the material from your class, you could help your friend develop a congruent attitude that she's also interested in the material from her classes.

A MIND READER'S PERSPECTIVE: HOW TO FREAK PEOPLE OUT USING THE IDEOMOTOR RESPONSE

Want to freak people out? Many psychological principles, such as the ideomotor response, can seem simplistic, but with enough showmanship, you can make these simplistic techniques seem like powerful miracles. This section describes one demonstration that you can use to truly freak people out.

43

First, find any pendulum type of object (an object attached to the end of a string that will swing back and forth). If you hold the end of the string steady and leave about eight inches of string for the object to swing freely in the air, you'll find that merely thinking about a direction will cause the object to swing in the direction that you're imagining. If you think about the pendulum swinging left and right, the pendulum will start swinging left and right. If you think about the pendulum swinging forward and back, it'll start swinging forward and back. Because of the ideomotor response, your hand will be making minuscule movements to move the pendulum, but the funny part is that you won't even feel your hand moving at all; it'll seem like you're controlling the pendulum with your mind. It's pretty freaky.

But here's where your showmanship can make this principle seem like a miracle. If you bring a pendulum to your friend, you can describe how that pendulum has certain "powers." To demonstrate, ask your friend to think of something (let's assume that you ask him to think of a playing card, and let's assume that he thinks of the Jack of Clubs). You instruct him to hold the end of the string so that the attached object hangs freely, and you explain that swinging forward and back means "yes" and that swinging left and right means "no."

After you give these basic instructions, you proceed to ask him yes or no questions about the playing card to narrow down the options, and you tell him to merely think of his answer. When he thinks of his answer, the pendulum will swing in the appropriate direction because of the ideomotor response, but your friend won't realize it. It'll seem like the pendulum is moving on its own.

For example, your first question could be, "Is your card red?" This would cause your friend to think "no" because his card is the Jack of Clubs. If you ask him to concentrate on his answer, the pendulum will start to move a little sporadically, but you'll find that it'll start to move consistently from side to side, indicating a negative answer.

You can then ask additional questions (e.g., Is your card a club? Is your card a royal card?) to narrow down the possibilities. After about five or six "yes" or "no" questions, you can divine the playing card that your friend never even mentioned out loud, and your friend will have no idea that it was the ideomotor response that caused the pendulum to swing in those directions. Though a simple principle, this demonstration can seem like a miraculous phenomenon to people.

44

REAL WORLD APPLICATION: HOW TO BOOST SALES

In this Real World Application, based on a study by Wansink, Kent, and Hoch (1998), you're a manager at a supermarket, and you decide to use anchoring, limitations (the topic of Chapter 13) and social pressure to boost sales of a particular item.

Near the shelves that display the cans of Campbell's soup, you hang a sign that says, "Limit of 12 per person." Albeit an innocent sign, that statement packs a powerful punch for a few reasons. First, the number 12 sets an anchor that people assimilate toward. Rather than purchase one or two cans, people are influenced by that anchor to purchase a larger number of cans. Second, as you'll learn in Chapter 13, limiting the ability to purchase those cans will spark "psychological reactance," and it'll spark a greater desire to purchase cans of soup. Third, that sign triggers social pressure by implying that the cans of soup are very popular (why else would the store be limiting the number of cans that people can purchase?).

In the actual study, the researchers included three variations of that sign, and they measured how many cans people purchased with each sign:

- "No limit per person" generated an average of 3.3 cans sold.
- "Limit of 4 per person" generated an average of 3.5 cans sold.
- "Limit of 12 per person" generated an average of 7.0 cans sold.

Remarkably, the original 12-limit sign generated sales that were nearly double those of the other signs.
If you wanted to further enhance the effectiveness of that sign, you could even change the wording to say, "Limit of 12 per customer" or "Limit of 12 per [Supermarket Name] customers." That small wording change takes advantage of ingroup favoritism by emphasizing that people from the same ingroup (i.e., customers) are purchasing those cans of soup. Much like the hotel influenced people to reuse their towels when they emphasized that guests from the same room did so, when you narrow the focus from "person" to "customer" or "[Supermarket Name] customers," you can exert even more pressure on people to purchase those cans of soup (or any other item for that matter).

8. The ability of the seller to listen to the customer. The techniques of active listening. Technique - How to ask the right questions to the client (which is interesting, the client may report and so on).

Use Repeated Exposures

If you had to guess, which picture of yourself do you think you'd prefer: an actual picture or a picture of your mirrored reflection? I'll give you a few paragraphs to think about it.

When I tried my first beer in college, I thought it tasted disgusting. I hated it. I started arguing with my friends because I thought they were crazy for enjoying the taste. They argued with me by saying that I would eventually learn to like it, but I still thought they were crazy.

It wasn't until my third or fourth beer until I finally realized that my friends were right. Although I initially hated my first few beers, I gradually developed an appreciation for the taste over time, and now I love the taste of beer. How could that be? How could something that I found so disgusting and repulsive become something that I now find very pleasant?

You've probably experienced similar situations in your own life. Have you ever heard a song for the first time that you immediately disliked? Then, after listening to it a few times, you actually began to enjoy it? How about when you meet someone for the first time? Maybe you dislike him at first, but after meeting him a few times, his personality starts to grow on you? These situations occur frequently, and they can be explained by a psychological principle.

The mere exposure effect, also known as the familiarity principle, suggests that we develop greater positive feelings toward a stimulus if we're repeatedly exposed to it. The more often you encounter a stimulus (e.g., beer, song, person), the more appealing and likable that stimulus generally becomes. Though it may appear counterintuitive to our current beliefs (such as the popular phrase, "familiarity breeds contempt"), ample evidence has shown that repeated exposures to a stimulus lead to a more favorable perception of that stimulus. This chapter sheds light on why that's the case.

THE POWER OF REPITITIONS

Now, back to my original question: do you think that you would prefer an actual picture of yourself or a picture of your mirrored reflection? Researchers conducted this experiment and found that, if presented with both options, you're more likely to prefer a picture of your mirrored reflection, whereas your friends are more likely to prefer the actual picture of yourself, even when those two images are virtually identical (Mita, Dermer, & Knight, 1977).

If you understand the mere exposure effect, you can understand why those results occurred. Think about it. Each day we wake up, walk into the bathroom, and what do we see? We see our reflection in the mirror. Each day we wake up, walk outside, and what do our friends see? They see us from their own viewing perspective. Therefore, when presented with those two images, people prefer the image that generates the most familiarity. We prefer the picture of our mirrored reflection, and our friends prefer the actual picture because those are the perspectives that generate the most familiarity.

Even if we fail to consciously notice a repeated stimulus, we're still likely to develop positive feelings toward it through nonconscious exposures. In one study, researchers repeatedly flashed geometric shapes to participants, and these shapes were flashed so quickly (4 milliseconds) that participants failed to consciously process them. After those exposures, the researchers presented participants with two shapes: one that was previously flashed and one that was completely new. The researchers asked them which shape they preferred, and despite absolutely no conscious recognition for the original shape, people consistently chose the shape that the researchers flashed on a nonconscious level (Bornstein, Leone, & Galley, 1987).

In fact, the mere exposure effect is stronger when the exposures occur non-consciously (Zajonc, 2001). How could something that we don't even perceive create a stronger effect? The answer lies in the affective primacy hypothesis, a concept suggesting that our emotional responses can be triggered before our cognitive responses. Mere exposure becomes stronger for exposures that occur outside of our conscious awareness because those exposures trigger an emotional response without triggering a cognitive response. They enhance mere exposure because whenever we consciously evaluate something, we attach other meanings and associations to that stimulus, thereby altering (and possibly degrading) our evaluation of it. Nonconscious exposures prevent those potentially harmful associations, and so they often produce more powerful effects than conscious exposures.

Ever since Robert Zajonc proposed the mere exposure effect in the 1960s (Zajonc, 1968), extensive research has investigated this phenomenon, and the results show that this effect applies in many different contexts with many different stimuli. The researchers who conducted the experiment with the geometric shapes conducted a follow-up study and replaced the shapes with pictures of actual people. They found that the results were consistent: participants who were repeatedly exposed to photographs of people on a nonconscious level consistently preferred those photographs over new photographs (Bornstein, Leone, & Galley, 1987). The next section explains why this effect occurs, and the remainder of the chapter will teach you specific techniques to apply that principle toward persuasion.

WHY ARE REPITITIONS SO POWERFUL?

The previous chapter described how similarities are powerful because of evolution; we're naturally drawn toward people who are similar because they pose less of a threat. The mere exposure effect works in a similar way, no pun intended. Repeated exposures can generate a positive attitude toward a stimulus because they promote a greater sense of familiarity with that stimulus, which makes that stimulus seem less threatening.

Besides evolution, however, there are a few other reasons why the mere exposure effect is so powerful. The two main explanations are classical conditioning and processing fluency (Zajonc, 2001). Because classical conditioning is described in the final chapter, this section will focus on processing fluency, a very interesting principle in psychology.

Processing Fluency. It might seem like a strange request, but you'll gain a much better understanding of processing fluency if you take a ew minutes to write a list of 12 specific instances in your life where ou acted assertively. Go ahead – I'll wait.

)o you have your list? Like most people, you probably thought of a few nstances very easily, but with each new example, you probably found t increasingly difficult to think of new instances. Surprisingly, that lifficulty in retrieval influenced how you perceived your level of ssertiveness. Researchers conducted that same exercise with people, xcept they asked one group to think of 12 instances, and they asked a lifferent group to think of only six instances. What do you think lappened when the researchers later asked those people to rate their wn assertiveness? Though you might be inclined to think that people vho listed 12 instances found themselves to be more assertive, the pposite actually occurred: people who listed only six instances viewed hemselves to be significantly more assertive than people who listed 12 nstances (Schwarz et al., 1991).

he explanation to that odd finding can be found in processing fluency - the ease and speed with which we process information (Reber, chwarz, & Winkielman, 2004). If you followed the exercise and listed 2 instances of your assertiveness, you likely experienced difficulty in enerating new instances the farther along you went. That perceived lifficulty is the answer. The difficulty you experienced in generating lew instances became a subtle cue that caused you to develop a ongruent attitude that you must not be assertive. You non-onsciously said, "Hmm. If I'm an assertive person, then I should have lo problem listing instances. But I am having trouble listing instances. herefore, I must not be assertive." The people who only listed six nstances, on the other hand, didn't experience as much difficulty enerating examples, so their nonconscious developed the opposite ttitude: "Hmm. If I'm an assertive person, then I should have no roblem listing instances. I'm not having trouble listing instances. herefore, I must be assertive."

he ease and speed with which we process information largely nfluences our perception of that information, including how much we ike it. Generally, the faster we're able to process information, the nore we tend to like that information. Why? When we're able to juickly process information, that ease of processing feels good, and we nisattribute the root cause of those positive feelings. When we xperience those positive feelings, we mistakenly believe that they are resulting from our fondness for the information, rather than our ease of processing (which is the actual cause).

How does that relate to repetitions? Repetitions are powerful because they increase processing fluency; each time that we view a repeated stimulus, we're able to process that stimulus more quickly the next time we encounter it.

It's like sledding down a snow-covered hill. The first time you try it you might not slide very fast because the snow won't be compacted. However, each time that you slide down the hill, those repetitions compact the snow and make a smoother pathway down the hill. As the snow becomes more compacted, the smoother your path becomes, and the faster you'll slide down the hill (and the faster you travel, the more you enjoy sledding down the hill).

Think of a time when you might've had the following experience. You start writing an essay and you immediately hate your writing. But after working on it for a few hours, you finally reach a point where you're pleased with it, and so you take a break for the rest of the day. When you return to it the next day, however, you find that you hate it again. Why is that?

The answer lies in processing fluency. You disliked the writing initially because your processing fluency was low; it was still foreign to you. But the more you worked on it, the more familiar it became, and the easier it became to process. You then misattributed the ease with which you processed it with your fondness for the writing. When you took a break from it, your processing fluency decreased, and because it wasn't as familiar to you when you returned to it, you weren't able to process it as easily. You then misattributed that difficulty in processing to a poor essay.

Now that you understand processing fluency and why repetitions are so powerful, the next section explains how you can use that concept to enhance your persuasion.

How can you take advantage of repetitions? This section offers a few suggestions.

Prime the Context. How pleasant do you find the word "boat"? It may seem like a weird question, but when researchers in one study asked people that same question, they found some interesting results. Compare the following two sentences that the researchers presented to two groups of people:

- He saved up his money and bought a boat.
- The stormy seas tossed the boat.

The researchers presented those two sentences to people and asked them to focus solely on the last word (i.e., "boat") and rate it on a pleasantness scale. Even though the question was essentially the same, people who were exposed to the second sentence rated "boat" to be significantly more pleasant (Whittlesea, 1993).

That result occurred because of conceptual fluency, a type of processing fluency related to how easily information comes to our mind (Alter & Oppenheimer, 2009). Generally, the faster a concept enters our mind, the more we tend to like it. Because the second sentence used particular words to prime the context, this heightened predictability caused the concept of "boat" to enter people's minds more easily, and that ease of processing produced a pleasant feeling that became misattributed to the word "boat."

Top-level marketers spend millions of dollars each year trying to take advantage of conceptual fluency. If we're deciding between two possible brands to purchase, we're likely to base our decision on how easily each brand comes to mind. When our opinion of two brands is the same, we're more likely to purchase the brand that comes to our mind more easily because that heightened conceptual fluency feels pleasant, and we mistakenly attribute that pleasantness to the brand (Nedungadi, 1990).

Marketers can take advantage of conceptual fluency and enhance the effectiveness of their advertisements by strategically positioning their ads in predictive contexts. For example, one study showed that consumers found a ketchup ad more favorable when the ad was

51

presented after an ad for mayonnaise (Lee & Labroo, 2004). The mayonnaise ad primed consumers' schema for condiments, and when the ad for ketchup was presented afterward, the idea of ketchup came to their minds more easily. As a result of that heightened conceptual fluency, consumers developed a more positive attitude toward the ketchup advertisement.

How can you apply that technique in your own life? You can increase your chances of persuading someone to comply with a request by casually mentioning the topic of your request immediately prior to making it. Similar to the mayonnaise ad, the general topic will increase your target's conceptual fluency for your request and, as a result, your request will seem more appealing because it will come to your target's mind more easily. Your target will then misattribute that ease of processing with a desire to comply with your request.

Suppose that your favorite band is coming to town, and you want to persuade your friend to go to the concert with you next month. However, your friend doesn't really like the band, so you expect to encounter some resistance. In this situation, don't rush and hastily make your request now; instead, periodically bring up the idea of concerts in general for the next few days. With repeated exposure to that general topic, your friend will gradually develop a more positive attitude toward concerts in general, and he will be less resistant when you make your actual request. Also, because of conceptual fluency, the idea of accompanying you to the concert will enter his mind more easily when you eventually make your request, and he will mistakenly attribute that higher conceptual fluency with a desire to go to the concert.

Use Any Repetitions. In addition to influencing our perception and behavior, repeated exposures by themselves enhance our general mood. Monahan, Murphy, and Zajonc (2000) subliminally exposed a group of participants to 25 Chinese ideographs (symbols and characters used in Chinese writing), and they exposed each ideograph only once. However, with a different group of participants, they exposed only five Chinese ideographs, but they repeated the exposures five times. Remarkably, compared to participants who were subliminally exposed to 25 different ideographs, participants who were exposed to the repeated ideographs were in better moods after the exposures.

Afterward, the researchers asked each group to evaluate a few different stimuli, including the same ideographs, similar ideographs, and new unrelated polygons. Compared to participants who were shown one exposure of 25 ideographs, and compared to a control group that wasn't exposed to any ideographs, participants who were exposed to the repeated ideographs evaluated all other stimuli more positively because of their enhanced mood. The conclusion: merely experiencing any form of repeated event or exposure can enhance our feelings in general, which can then lead to greater positive feelings toward other stimuli that we encounter.

Have you noticed that all of the chapter titles in this book use a similar wording style? Every chapter title uses a sequence of three words (with an action verb as the first word), and this style is repeated for every chapter. Each time that you begin a new chapter and become exposed to that repeated wording style, your ease of processing that title can put you in a better mood, which can lead you to perceive the contents of that chapter more favorably.

Create Greater Proximity. If you were attending a college class in a large lecture hall with hundreds of students, would you remember every person from that class at the end of the semester? Probably not. But even if you don't remember a specific person, research shows that having been in the mere proximity of someone can create a favorable perception of that person.

Two researchers conducted a neat field experiment to test that claim (Moreland & Beach, 1992). The researchers asked four female students to be confederates in an experiment, and their job was to attend a predetermined number of classes in a psychology course (0, 5, 10 or 15 classes). Because they were instructed not to interact with other students, and because the classes were held in a large lecture hall, their presence was unnoticed by most students.

At the end of the semester, the researchers showed students a picture of each confederate that attended the class, and they asked the students to evaluate the four females. Despite possessing only vague memories, if any, for those confederates, students perceived the confederates to be more similar and attractive with the more classes they attended. When we're in the mere general vicinity of someone more often, that person is likely to find us more attractive!

Sure, you may be thinking, people might prefer a photograph if they've been exposed to it before. Heck, people might even find someone more attractive if they are repeatedly exposed to that person. But is this effect strong enough to influence our actual behavior?

Good question. Repeated exposures, even if they occur non-consciously, can exert tremendous influence on our behavior as well. Remember the researchers who conducted the experiment with the geometric shapes? They conducted a follow-up experiment where they instructed people to read anonymous poems and collaborate with two other participants to make a unanimous decision regarding the gender of the anonymous poet. However, only one person was an actual participant in the experiment; the other two people were confederates hired by the researchers. They were instructed to disagree with each other, which would force the actual participant to then choose a side.

Before those discussions occurred, the genuine participants were repeatedly flashed with one of three pictures: a blank picture, a picture of Confederate A, or a picture of Confederate B (similar to the previous studies, these stimuli were flashed so quickly that participants failed to consciously notice them). The researchers wanted to examine how those nonconscious exposures would influence their interactions with the two confederates, and the results were startling.

Among participants who were flashed with a neutral blank picture, roughly 50 percent agreed with Confederate A, and 50 percent agreed with Confederate B, an expected even split. When participants were repeatedly flashed with a photograph of Confederate B prior to the discussion, 65 percent of participants agreed with Confederate B, and only 35 percent agreed with Confederate A. But when participants were instead flashed with a photograph of Confederate A, 71 percent of participants agreed with Confederate A, and only 29 percent agreed with Confederate B (Bornstein, Leone, & Galley, 1987). Repeated exposures not only influence our perception of a stimulus (e.g., someone's level of attractiveness), but can also influence our actual behavior, a very helpful notion when it comes to persuasion.

9. Universal methods of persuasion. How to show the benefit in favor of the buyer.

Objection management is part and parcel of any sales process. Objections rear their seemingly ugly heads right from the first time you meet a client and, at times, many continue to torment you even after the product is sold. For a good salesperson, objections are seen not as obstacles but as business opportunities. If a customer is spending time to illustrate an objection, it means your customer is an interested party and the chances of a closed sale are high.

Objections, broadly, are divided into a few strategic categories and some of them are:

- I am happy with a similar product from your competitor.
- Send me information on mail and I will revert to you.
- I am not at all interested. Do not bother me.
- I need this but right now it is not a priority.
- Your pricing is high.

Irrespective of what the objections are, remember the following points in managing and handling them:

➢ <u>Prepare yourself for the objections</u>. Make copious notes, create virtual solutions, brainstorm with colleagues and do everything that is needed to ensure that you have answers to most of the expected objections of your product(s). For this, you need to know your products inside and out. Practice your answer, preferably with a colleague. Do not make calls without knowing your products really well. This will ensure that, more often not, you are ready with an emphatic answer for most of the questions.

➢ <u>Show gratitude for the objection raised by the customer</u>. Always thank the customer first when he raises an objection. You must remember that objections are pathways to a successful deal closure and gratitude for such opportunities must be exhibited.

➢ <u>Empathize with your customer</u>. When you empathize with your customer, you connect at a very personal level. Listen intently and show that you understand and care for his comments and objections. Use "I'm sorry you feel like that," "I understand your frustration," "I know how you feel but I think I can help you with that," and more such empathizing language. Beware of getting defensive about your product; this attitude will only enhance the divide between you and your customer.

> Get down to brass tacks. Once the emotional angle has been managed, you can work towards the details of the objection and here is where your preparing sessions will come in extremely handy. Rephrase the same question so that you get answers that tell exactly what objections and issues the customer has. Remember to build a good rapport during the discussion phase. Do not convert it into an argumentative process wherein you are trying to prove yourself right. Remember you do not need to be right; you just need to close the deal for yourself.

> Emphasize the value in your products. For sustained customer loyalty, remember to show them what value your product delivers. The process of customer discovery includes knowing what he needs from your product and how you can present it in a way that he relates to. Use various irrefutable proofs to emphasize the value in your product.

A few effective answers for common objections:

I am happy with a similar product from your competitor. Respond by focusing on the unique aspects of your product and other value-added services not included in the competitor's product.

Send me information via email and I will revert to you. While you confirm/ask for the correct email ID, give specific options including day and time. Or ask which days and/or times are convenient for him. These questions will ensure that the lead remains active and you can follow up later.

I am not interested at all; do not bother me. These clear-cut shutdown statements require experienced handling skills. You have to probe gently and find out what your customer's real interests are and then take it forward. Let the customer see your genuine curiosity and concern when he opens up with further objections.

Pricing. This is possibly the most basic and unavoidable objection of any sale. There are research reports that reveal most price objections are phony, meaning the customer is not interested in the pricing as much as he is interested in knowing what exactly he is saving through your product. Be ready with answers! As these questions are expected, you can easily prepare for them and handle them such that pricing issue never comes back during any discussion.

Like most difficult things in the world, managing objections requires patience and plenty of practice. You will see your confidence and capabilities increasing with every call and customer interaction. Your seniors and your colleagues are your support system. Leverage the experiences of your seniors and share learning experiences with your colleagues and see yourself becoming a pro sooner than later.

Always present your product in the way your customer wants to see it and not necessarily in the way you see it. Be patient with your customer, build a good rapport with him and discover his needs – all of these will make you an effective salesperson and your customer's loyalty will be assured.

10. The Socrates method of questions (this is the method of conversation that Socrates used describes this technique)

By understanding your customer's mind better, you have a much higher chance of success than without knowing their psychological working.

You need to know how to use psychology to convince, persuade and influence people such that they buy your products. Understanding the psychological principles that influence people will empower your sales campaigns like never. Here are some basic principles that will help you to use psychology in your selling:

- Law of Reciprocity
- Social Proof
- Commitment and Consistency
- Authority

- Liking
- Demand for scarcity

Let us look at each one in a little detail so that you comprehend its meaning.

Law of Reciprocity. This states that we feel compelled to return an obligation we received. For example, if your colleague took your side when you presented your project for the team, then you feel obligated to take his/her side when the time comes.

You can use this principle very effectively in marketing and increase your sales numbers. Clearly know what your objectives are and what you need from your customers. Be aware of what you can give in return.

There is an influence model designed by Cohen-Bradford that is based on this law of reciprocity (which is founded on a philosophy that most of us can relate to; all things good or bad you do unto others will come back to you). The Cohen-Bradford influence model is a great model to use in your marketing strategy. Its principles are as follows:

Treat everyone as a friend – an excellent place to start. Do not think of anyone as an antagonist. What happens when you treat all as friends is you begin to ooze positivity and even if the other person's enthusiasm does not match yours, there will not be any ill will.

Keep your objective clear in your head. Why and how are you going to influence the person you are interacting with? Can you get something in return for what you have to offer? When the point of exchange is arrived at unequivocally, no other obstacle can prevent the closure of the sale.

Look at things from the other person's perspective. Two critical positives can come out of this: the first is you empathize with the other side's worries and anxieties, and the second is you get a second outlook, which gives you more conducive business opportunity than before. This is because you will now be empowered to present your product in the way the other person wants to see it! What can stop you now?

Social Proof. It is common knowledge among salesmen that people tend to buy things that are recommended by friends and family, trust being the binding factor. Ensure your product has links to all popular social media networks so that your existing customers can tell their friends and family about it on their favorite platform and word gets around about your brand.

Commitment and Consistency. This is another attitude of human behavior that you can leverage to increase sales. The principle states that if you have committed to something, you are more likely to live up to your word rather than go against your word. This is true even if later your decision seems irrational to you.

How to leverage this? Find a way to get potential customers to commit to you even if it is something as small as sharing their personal email so that you can send promotional content directly to them. The chance that this seemingly small commitment will convert into an actual sale is very high. Other examples include a postponement of the deal for a fixed time in the future, a commitment to see the next product that you are developing and more.

Authority. The power that an authoritative person wields on the human mind is huge. For a school child, the teacher is a form of authority and hence the child will not easily refute whatever he or she says. For a subordinate, a boss is seen as a form of authority and this drives the boss to get things done by people reporting to him.

The fact that such power of authority was and has been misused by unscrupulous people all over the world (despite the negative connotations) reiterates the immense potency of authoritative power. You can use this power in your sales pitch. If, for example, your product has a scientific background, include videos and content from professionals. This will add a lot of weight to your product.

Liking. This is a primary psychological reason as to why brands get celebrities to endorse products. We love to buy things that we can connect with. Be it a smiling model, a popular actor or a sportsperson, when we see products used by people we like, we tend to buy those products for ourselves.

Your product must tell a story to its target audience, one that the audience will "like." If your products are for little children, let there be a warm and colorful story; if your product is for macho men, let the story be of well-bodied hunks; if your product is for women, let the feminine charm seep through your story. Importantly, the story you relate to your products must be "liked" by the target audience for an increasing enriching bottom line.

Demand for scarcity. The basis on which this psychological principle works is that when we think or know that a product is going to be scarce or we might lose a chance to buy it, we desire it more than if it was freely available. That is the reason why rare metals such as platinum are so expensive even if the shine on them appears far less than other more easily available metals.

How should you use this principle in your sales pitch? Let people know that the items on sale are not going to be available at all times. Add an exclusivity touch to your products, like an exclusive edition with a couple of great features that will not be seen in future models. Other successful tactics include short-term discounts for popular items and limited stock clearance sales. You can come up with your own idea to leverage this principle of demand for scarcity.

While the above six principles help you understand consumer behavior, there are some psychological obstacles that can work against your leadership qualities if you are not conscious of them. And here are a few psychological aspects that you need to be aware of with respect to yourself and your team:

- Bias
- Emotional quotient
- Support/Anchor
- Enjoying the process
- Using associative thinking ability

Bias. If you are deeply attached to your products/innovations, you might run the risk of not seeing and hence not be able to correct the flaws. Allow trusted people and professional experts to access, check and verify the veracity of your products. You could end up releasing a wrongly or badly designed product and your entrepreneurial efforts will not deliver the goods.

Emotional Quotient. You must hone your abilities to read people's non-verbal gestures and truly comprehend their needs. This will go a long way in creating products that meet and exceed your customers' needs. Moreover, gaining this skill will give you the power to know whether people are disguising their true feelings behind empty words. And this is indeed a powerful tool that you can use for the success of your venture.

Support/Anchoring Needs. Most of us rely on older and proven experiences to make decisions of any kind. While these kinds of anchor lines help us in living a smooth and contentedly comfortable life, for innovation this attitude could actually be a huge hindrance. You must be able to break a few conventional shackles, think out of the box, and get outside your comfort zone to make innovation a success, which in turn will make your business a success. Use anchor lines wisely and be prepared to let go of some of them, especially those that are retarding growth.

Enjoying the Process. Having fun while you innovate is the key to producing good results. Happiness, along with an element of fun, is great motivation for product designers, creators, sales force and employees at large. Keep your work environment colorful, pleasant and enjoyable to get best results.

Using an associative thinking ability. When you are stumped with an obstacle, remembering a similar situation and creating solutions based on those experiences is called associative thinking. This way of solving problems is reflective of an astute leadership. Work towards developing and honing such a skill to enhance the success of your business.

Psychology plays a very important part in making a success of your business venture. Learn and discern techniques that hinder and accelerate the growth process of your company. Minimize the hindrances and maximum the accelerators and watch your profits expand exponentially.

11. Method 80/20 sales and marketing.

One day in the summer of 1873, the town of Bloomington, Illinois wa abuzz with excitement at the arrival of Barnum's Travelling World' Fair. At that time, there were numerous traveling circuses in the US but P.T. Barnum's was the biggest and the best. The circus wa considered a "miracle of enterprise" and one of the "eight wonders o the world." It featured "freaks and curiosities... wild men from ever uncivilized quarter of the globe," rare animals from the jungles of Asi and Africa, and the leading equestrians and acrobats of the day.

The arrival of the circus into town was announced by a massive parad where musicians, performers and animals in full costume rode ato parade vans and cages. And on that hot July day, Perley Silloway, budding and youthful circus fan, was so inspired by the wonder of P.T Barnum's circus that he would later go on to operate his own one-rin circus in Illinois. Reflecting back years later, what stood out fo Silloway in the circus was not the circus acts themselves. Instead, wha was imprinted in his memory was the **tremendous crowd** i attendance. There were thousands of people in the show grounds pushing and shoving around the ticket wagon. There were specia excursion trains that had brought hundreds of people from outlyin areas into the city for the shows. Papers the next day reported tha 2000 people were turned away as the evening show performed to th sell-out crowd.

The circus offered the best form of entertainment at the time, but it true success lay behind the great P.T. Barnum himself, who knev better than anyone that "nothing attracts a crowd like a crowd. Perhaps one of the greatest promoters of all time, he knew that if h could create enough excitement and energy among his fans, th excitement itself would draw ever larger crowds to his shows. And thi is how the term 'Bandwagon Effect' came to be known.

Almost two centuries later, P.T. Barnum's Bandwagon Effect ha become a key concept in explaining how people are drawn to crowd and to whatever's new on the market. It explains why we find a crowc camped out in front of Apple stores on the eve of a new produc launch. It's behind the success of every boy band. It even explains th behavior of voters who seem to have an innate desire to support

winner, as illustrated by the cases of John Kerry in 2004 and Donald Trump in the lead-up to the 2016 US presidential election.
But how does the *Bandwagon Effect* happen?

The human brain is like a remarkable living computer that is constantly taking in copious amounts of data, far more than it can process, while simultaneously functioning normally throughout the day. As the brain references the incoming data against its own data bank of schemas, it biases us to respond to certain situations based on partial data without critically evaluating every situation we encounter. Known as cognitive biases, these explain how we adopt beliefs about ourselves and the world to justify our behavior and decisions.

Often, these cognitive biases serve us well. Consider those 'fanboys' who are led by the *Bandwagon Effect* to camp out in front of their Apple store for the latest phone launch. They end up with a high-quality device, which, accordingly to the American Customer Satisfaction Index, has a higher percentage of satisfied customers than most other brands. There are instances, however, when our brains don't serve us well. It is easy to be blinded by the popular draw of a politician even when the reality is that there is not enough substance behind the soundbites and catch phrases used in their speeches.

As salespeople, the *Bandwagon Effect* is just one of a whole host of psychological concepts influencing the behavior of those around you. When you understand even just a little of the psychology at play during the sales process, you possess a great advantage. By understanding the biases and effect on both individuals and groups, you can strengthen your arguments, anticipate your customers' and clients' reactions, and connect powerfully with your market.

In this book I share with you some of the ways you can use these biases to connect with people and close your sales. But more than that, I hope that this book might trigger changes in your own life in the way you handle interactions with other people – from your boss to colleagues, friends and family.

I want to stress that this book is not intended to assist you in manipulating others! Instead, the goal of this book is to help you create an environment for your customers that optimizes the possibility of their making ***mutually-beneficial*** decisions that they might otherwise be unable to make. Oftentimes, for some salespeople, closing a sale can be tantamount to cheating, manipulating the customers or providing some false claims. Throughout this book, the emphasis on providing excellent customer service prevails. No matter what 'tricks and strategies' one uses to shape the thoughts and behavior of the customer, essential things such as quality products, outstanding service and a salesperson with integrity will still always outperform in the long haul.

Every day, we seek to change other people's behaviors to meet our own needs. At times this can be deliberate and at other times it's an unconscious exercise. As salespeople, we might as well be organized about it.

12. How to increase your confidence.

In 2008, some 300,000 Chinese babies got sick from milk formula that contained melamine, which had been added by the manufacturer in a bid to reduce material costs. When the scandal broke, there was widespread consumer panic. Sales of local milk products dropped by 30–40 percent as the Chinese public started to doubt whether other brands were also safe. Mothers switched to imported formula milk. Needless to say, it also affected China's reputation as a world manufacturer of goods. Even now, there's still the occasional joke about drinking milk products made from China.

When a major tragedy like this happens, they can stick in people's minds and become, in a way, a critical factor when people make judgments or decisions. The same can be said of events such as a plane crash. If news of an airline crash breaks, we hear about the sudden drop in flight bookings as customers become slightly careful or afraid and more likely to postpone their trip, or forgo the idea of flying in the immediate future.

These conditions can be attributed to what we call the *Availability Heuristic*, a form of bias where the mind relies on immediate, recent or memorable information or memory to make a decision. When we are considering a decision, certain situations or events come to mind and because they were the things that first occurred to us, we tend to believe that there is greater likelihood and possibility of the same event or situation happening. Our decision is then made based on how positive (or negative) our memory is of that event or situation.

How We Can Make the Availability Heuristic Work in Sales

In a simplistic sense, the *Availability Heuristic* means that good and positive images or memory can influence positive decisions, and uncomfortable and negative ones can have negative outcomes. So, if we want our clients to remember us, then we need to paint a vivid, positive and memorable image of our business that they can easily remember when they're making a decision. How? Here are a few ideas:

- ***Provide them with something from your business that will stand out.*** This could be a simple handwritten thank-you note, a jaw-dropping presentation, a colorful brochure, a rocking personal description on your calling card, or a personalized treatment during a meeting.

- ***Remember to repeat key ideas.*** Repetition is an essential tool for recall. Nike's "Just Do It" slogan that the company blankets across all forms of advertising media is short, catchy and easy to remember.

- ***Use stories to create mental pictures.*** Powerful images are best rendered in stories, whether positive (to motivate) or negative (to instill fear of loss). If you're delivering a presentation to a prospective client, you can present the features of your products using testimonials or stories from previous clients and customers.

The more vivid the mental picture you create for your business, the stronger the mental recall on your customers. When you stick in their minds with a positive, memorable image, there's an excellent chance they'll consider you in their list of options.

It is not your customer's job to remember you. It is your obligation and responsibility to make sure they don't have the chance to forget you. ~Patricia Fripp

13. The right attitude to their work.

As someone who has worked in sales and marketing for years, I have heard lines such as "There was something about the product that called out to me" or "I can absolutely relate." I've seen how sales have spiked with a single story, line or picture that customers found relatable to them.

A good example is Apple. Before its current "Think different" slogan, one of the company's winning ad lines was "Macintosh – the computer for the rest of us." The message conveys the idea of a technology that is inclusive and designed for everyone, with the use of the collective "us" speaking directly to customers. Years after this slogan was used, Apple continues to be one of the most preferred laptop brands of all ages.

This is what we call the power of personal connection. Adrian Miller, a sales trainer in New York, explains that people support a brand that "they like and can relate to." And it is this personal connection, established by the salesperson through constant contact over time, that turns first-time buyers into loyal customers. When such personal connection is lost, customers turn to someone else.

Making Connections with Customers More Personal

How do you make connections with your clients and customers more personal? Here are a few ways:

- *Increase your likeability by adding value first.* A personal brand is a likable brand, and one of the ways to enhance your likeability is to provide some added value that will interest and entice your clients. Promotions such as free gift coupons, free trials or easy returns are some ways you can add value.

- *Meet with them in person.* Email and phone conversations may be the "in" thing now because they're convenient and easy, but face-to-face meetings still remain one of the most genuine forms of communication for building personal connections. Arranging a face-to-face meeting with a new client can pay dividends for the long term relationship.

- ***Know something personal about your clients.*** Customers do not just want to know that they are appreciated; they also want to know that they're not seen as walking dollar signs who can bring business to a company.

Laurie Brown, author of *The Greet Your Customer Manual*, advises that one way to establish deeper personal connections with customers is to know a couple personal things about them. Something as simple as the food they like, a coffee shop they frequent, or their favorite weekend pastime can come in handy when setting up meetings or sending that email follow-up.

Most of all, remember that building personal connections is not a one-time thing. It is not something that takes place only at the initial contact but rather, throughout the business relationship. When customers know they're getting personalized service and are valued, they will stick with you.

14. Correct attitude towards clients.

Elizabeth Newton, a graduate of Stanford University, wanted to know how many of the things that we know are also known by others. She designed a simple experiment where she asked one person to tap the rhythm of a song and another to guess the song. In the experiment, the listeners were only able to guess three out of the 120 songs tapped while the tappers assumed that the listeners could recognize at least half of the songs. If this finding can be applied to the real world, it's entirely possible that other people only know 2.5% of what we think they know!

When something is so familiar to us, we tend to talk about it dismissively, expecting others to know what we're talking about. The reality, though, is that they may understand only very little of what we're saying – or even none at all. This is what we call the *Curse of Knowledge*, something that we, as salespeople may be guilty of in our interactions with clients and customers.

Getting Swallowed in Jargon

How many times have we seen or heard IT companies use big words like "optimization of business infrastructure," "server build and support," or "network implementation"? If you were to ask their prospects and customers what these terms mean, how many do you think would be able to explain them? Most likely not many, if any.

As salespeople, we have been trained to acquire mastery of the company and our products to be able to confidently answer questions. However, this expert knowledge may be lost in translation in our interactions with our customers and clients. Too often, salespeople ramble on about the product, using technical language that they expect customers to know because the language is common in the industry. Then they feel helpless when customers don't understand their explanation.

Avoiding the Curse of Knowledge

The cardinal rule is to first be aware of where your customer is on the knowledge curve. Some customers may be experts, others may have minimal understanding, and others have zero knowledge. Checking with your customers on how much they know of your business or your product is a good place to start. Likewise, when talking about benefits or solutions with your customers, it is best to be specific.

Don't settle for vague or ambiguous descriptions. When you ask customers, for example, what is a quality product or solution for them, ask them to describe or quantify.

Use the descriptions they provided to describe your product. During your presentation, listen for the vocabulary that the prospect uses to describe your product or service and build these terms into your pitch. This serves a two-pronged purpose of showing them that your product is the solution they need and confirming their own descriptions.

Use stories. Anecdotes and stories are not only personal, but they also make your brand even more genuine and believable and this gives customers an experience that they can relate to.

The *Curse of Knowledge* intimidates customers and clients, and when they are intimidated, we risk losing the connection we've built with them. Customers fail to make the connection between their problem and the product we're marketing as the solution, resulting in a failed sales pitch. So the next time you're talking to a client or a customer, ask yourself: "Am I getting through?"

Aim for brevity while avoiding jargon. ~ Edsger Dijkstra

15. Conclusion.

In summary, by reading this book, you should now have the required basic skills to succeed in the sales industry. We have learned that sales is a personalized process that differs from marketing, and successful salespeople share five traits: discipline, tenacity, implementation, focus and desire. We have also learned that when we ask for the sale, we should be asking a question that forces the customer give a reason for why they are not going to buy today. This way, you can explore with the customer ways that you can overcome this objection.

This book has also shown you the various sales tools and sales strategies that will allow you to effectively develop your business into a very successful organization, and the key to this cultivation depends on building long-lasting relationships with our customers by asking quality and relevant questions. Lastly, we looked at some simple cold-calling techniques you can use to increase your sales conversion rate when making phone calls to potential customers.

Use this book as a guide and reference on your journey to becoming a successful salesperson, and always remember that it is up to each one of us to make the decision to be successful. Come back and read this book any time you need to refresh your skills or need motivation or inspiration, as it will ensure success in your future.

www.ingramcontent.com/pod-product-compliance
Lightning Source LLC
Chambersburg PA
CBHW071232220526
45468CB00002B/819